Guidelines for Finding a

Christian Husband

TINA LOUISE RISTINE

© 2004 by Tina Louise Ristine. All rights reserved

Packaged by Pleasant Word, PO Box 428, Enumclaw, WA 98022. The views expressed or implied in this work do not necessarily reflect those of Pleasant Word. The author(s) is ultimately responsible for the design, content and editorial accuracy of this work.

No part of this publication may be reproduced, stored in a retrieval system or transmitted in any way by any means—electronic, mechanical, photocopy, recording or otherwise—without the prior permission of the copyright holder, except as provided by USA copyright law.

Unless otherwise noted, all Scriptures are taken from the Holy Bible, New International Version, Copyright © 1973, 1978, 1984 by the International Bible Society. Used by permission of Zondervan Publishing House. The "NIV" and "New International Version" trademarks are registered in the United States Patent and Trademark Office by International Bible Society.

ISBN 1414-0130-9
Library of Congress Catalog Card Number: 2004100713

This book is dedicated to my father, Lee Davidson, whose encouragement inspired me to be all that God intended for me to be and for my mother, Christine Davidson, who helped to fund this book that God inspired me to write.

Contents

Chapter 1

The Importance of Family in Choosing a Mate

The number One guideline in finding a Christian husband is to notice how he treats his mother or sister, especially his mother. This is a good indicator as to how he will treat you as his future wife. Also it is important to note how your intended spouse's father treats his wife. However, if his parents are deceased, the time invested in getting to know the rest of his family is vital. He will be much like the family that he comes from!

Spending the holidays with his family also will allow you to get to know him better. Holidays can be a stressful time. We can easily get caught up in the number of people to see and the presents to buy that we sometimes forget to return to ourselves for a reprieve. Be certain to schedule some time out of the busyness to be alone just the two of you doing some special activity that you both enjoy like a walk in the park or along the beach.

Be sure to reconnect with yourselves as individuals enjoying your hobbies and again with each other as a couple. Make pleasant memories for both of you to cherish in years to come. Make sure that you either keep a camera handy or a notebook to journal in your special memories as a couple.

Chapter 2

Group Dating

Develop time getting to know one another in Christian circles. After church or after a Christian singles' meeting, start dating him in groups. This way you get to see the way your prospective spouse relates to others. You can determine if you are special to him or just one of the other gals in the group.

Once you do become married, your friends become his friends. Don't waste your time trying to get your friends before you were married to like your new spouse. Let them cultivate the friendship on their own. I know that it is tempting to intervene and make them like each other. This has much more to do with our need to feel important than it does with helping our new spouse.

Chapter 3

Dating Techniques

Once a week, spend time alone together with him. Dating should be like a job interview. You want to find the best candidate for the job of lifetime partner. Write down at least 10 questions to ask him about his character and hobbies per date. Take notes and pray over your date/future mate. The time invested now may save a possible heartache in the future.

Chapter 4

Developing Common Interest

Take the time to develop common interests. If one of you enjoys the outdoors and the other one gets an allergic reaction to the outdoors, this is not a common point to focus on. However, if both of you enjoy going to the movies, find a movie that both of you will enjoy! The more common interest you have, the better your relationship will be as there will be less disagreements upon which activities to engage in. When you embark in marriage a journey is promised. The more that you give to your lifelong partner, the more he will want to give back to you.

Start developing a marriage mentality before you get married. Learn to think of yourself as an individual and as a whole. Do things with your intended spouse together that you enjoy and also do things that you enjoy apart from him. What you do during your free time developing outside interests should make you feel free. Once you are married your energies will be poured into creating your identity as a couple.

Remember that your prospective partner's idea of intimacy may be very different from yours. Try intimacy his way and keep an open mind. Remember to honor his idea of intimacy as you wish him to honor your idea of intimacy. Reserve sex for the marriage bed only!

There is a common saying in relationships that "Opposites do attract." This really only applies to science where north and south poles attract and like poles repel. Only do opposite strengths and weaknesses compliment each other. For example, my mother is very frugal with her money; My Dad, on the other hand, is a spendthrift. This trait, however, complimented each other in the rearing of their nine children.

However, I do strongly believe that the more common interests that you develop together as a couple, the more likely that your marriage will be successful. If, for example, you both have an interest in computers, you can help and teach each other in this area. The reality is that the more common interests you two shares, the more likely that your marriage will succeed! Taking the time now getting to know if the two of you are compatible with one another is vital and so is having common interests!

15

Chapter 5

Cooking For Him

Find out your prospective mates favorite foods and cook a romantic, candlelit dinner for him. The saying that "The way to a man's heart is through his stomach" (author unknown) is not far from the truth! However, I recommend that you get to know him about sixth months before you decide to cook him his favorite dinner. This is a very intimate activity, as you will both be alone in either his or your home and you want to make sure that you've discussed your physical boundaries first. Make sure that you both have an agreement upon your physical boundaries first before trying this approach.

Chapter 6

Your Value System

Find out your intended mates value system. Look for someone who has a similar value system as you do. This will be especially important if you are planning on rearing children. Nothing confuses children more than if their parents can not agree on important issues of life such as creation vs. evolution, nature vs. nurture theories, and where to attend church. You do not have to agree upon everything, just the major issues of life!!

Chapter 7

Being Particular

The most important thing to remember is that no one is perfect. You should have your standards high. For example, if you would only consider dating someone who does not have children from a prior marriage, do not lower your standards for anyone. Be choosy; it will pay off for you in the long run!

Chapter 8

Developing Boundaries in Dating

Do not become overly physically intimate too soon in the relationship. Relationships take time and energy. If you become too close right away physically, you will not get to know your prospective mate in other ways. You will not get to know how he makes decisions, how he manages his money, and other valuable area. Take the time to get to know him as a person not just a body!

Withhold sexual intercourse from him until you both say "I Do." Men respect someone who does not come too easily. If you give him something that he strongly desires such as sex, chances are that he will never marry you. Secondly, it cheapens God-given sexual intimacy, which should be reserved for the marriage bed only. If you're not good enough in his eyes for him to marry you, having sex with him will not convince him to marry you!

Set up physical boundaries when you're dating. In other words, don't just show up at his home. He may get the wrong impression. Also, do not put yourself in moral tempting situations. Do not compromise your values for him and he will respect you more!

Chapter 9

Avoiding Dangerous Men

Make sure that your prospective mate is not an angry man. This is an outward expression of a much larger problem, which you are not qualified to solve. It is also a symptom of an abusive man. As Proverbs states in Chapter 22:24–25 "Do not make friends with a hot-tempered man, do not associate with one easily angered, or you may learn his ways and get yourself ensnared" . Only by getting to know your prospective partner over time will you be able to discern if he carries around a lot of anger!

Chapter 10

Developing Financial Freedom Together

*M*ake sure that your prospective partner has financial freedom. Bringing a lot of debt into a relationship is not a good way to get a solid foundation. A good guideline to follow is the make sure that he has not only a good job but also has at least 3 times his salary in savings for family emergencies. I am not recommending that you marry a millionaire such as Bill Gates but someone who has followed Scriptural injunction: "To Owe No man anything except to Love one Another" (Romans 13:8).

Once you've married him, you must have some agreement over finances. Money is a touchy area for some people so make sure you reach a resolution that both of you can live with. Discuss this in advance to getting married. For example, some people may keep their finances separate and split expenses down the middle like I did in my first marriage. This did not work too well for me; however, as it seemed like we just could not make ends meet. Another solution could mean that the two of you merge accounts completely. For other people it may mean a combination of the two ideas. Whatever you decide, make sure that you both agree comfortably.

Money may be handled in different ways at different times in your marriage. You should agree upon in advance who will write out which bills. You must have a certain level of trust in your partner to not only write out the bills you two share but also to allow you a spend able income if only he works.

However, as the economic balance between you changes as you re-enter the work force, expect questions of money to arise. Assume that there will be heated discussions about money between the two of you. Trust will need to develop in the area of money or it will tear you apart as a couple. Money symbolizes power in your marriage. As King Solomon states it clearly in Ecclesiastes 10:19 "A feast is made for laughter, and wine makes life merry, but money is the answer for everything".

Chapter 11

Developing a Sense of Humor

Make sure that you're prospective mate has a sense of humor. When life's tragedies happen, as they will, it is important to be able to laugh at yourself. There is a difference between laughing at someone else and being able to laugh at your own mistakes. Tell your prospective partner one of your funniest jokes and notice his response. Spend time also laughing with your partner. Learn to laugh together even during difficult times.

Chapter 12

Looking For Integrity

Make sure that your prospective partner is a man of integrity. Believe me; nothing is worse than being married to a habitual liar. If you cannot trust his word now when you are dating, it will not change just because you said the two infamous words "I DO." Only time will tell if he is a man of integrity; you will not be able to find this one out overnight or in a short period of time.

Learn to allow your future spouse to be himself. If he is doing something that seems irresponsible or dangerous, it is your responsibility to let him know, but you cannot change him. Allow him to be himself and bless him for who he is.

Chapter 13

Taking Your Time

Personally, I recommend that you date a minimum of one year before you consider marriage. The reasons are that most men will put their best foot forward and will prevent you from seeing their weaknesses during this time period. As the saying goes, "Love Is Often blind" (author unknown). Secondly, I want to observe my prospective partner in a variety of situations, such as how he worships at church, how he relates to others at work, at home, in his peer group, how he treats other women in my presence or better yet how he treats me when other women are around. Am I special to him or am I just a sidekick? Take the time to get to know now because as the saying goes: if I "Marry in Haste; I will Repent in leisure" (quote by Lee Davidson, my father).

Chapter 14

Dating Generous Men

Make sure that your prospective partner is a generous man. Nothing could be worse than being married to a penny-pincher or to one who can squeeze the blood out of a nickel! Proverbs 23:6–8 states it clearly: "Do not eat the food of a stingy man, do not crave his delicacies; for he is the kind of man who is always thinking about the cost. 'Eat and drink,' he says to you, but his heart is not with you."

Chapter 15

Dating a Mature Christian

This item really should be number one on your list of whom to marry. Make sure that he loves the Lord and attends church regularly. If he is involved in the local body, chances are that he is a growing Christian. You do not want to marry just a Christian man; you want to marry a "Growing" Christian, young man.

Chapter 16

Dating "Attractive" Men

*M*ake sure that he is well kept. By this I do not mean financially only but also I mean to make sure that he is well groomed. Remember that, "he who loves his wife loves himself" (Ephesians 5:28). You want to make certain that he loves himself so he can also love the extension of himself: You, as his wife.

Date and marry a man who is reasonably healthy physically. If, for example, he has a heart disease chances are you will not only have to quit your job to care for him, but also you will outlive him. If this does not bother you, then great! However, if you do not want to be a widow early on in your marriage, then back out of the "love game" with him!

Chapter 17

Is He a Leader?

Make certain that your prospective mate is a leader. Can he lead others who will follow his Godly lifestyle? The husband is the head of the wife as Christ is the head of the church (Ephesians 5:23). Remember, Too that you are not looking for a dictator, but one who will lead you gently to follow in the image of Christ.

Chapter 18

Can He Compromise?

*M*ake sure that your prospective partner knows how to compromise. If he insists on getting his way all the time, be wary. This is a symptom of a much-deeper problem possibly reared its ugly head in childhood. For example, when he asks you where you want to eat you could say something like "I prefer Vietnamese food but I'm open to your preference." If he takes you to Vietnamese food, then you know that he has the ability to compromise. It may take you asking him several times where he would like to eat also before you can determine if he has the ability to compromise. You may also ask him which types of movies he enjoys watching. Tell him your preference such as love stories, for example, and if the next time he suggests a love story that should tell you that he knows how to compromise.

Once you are married, it is important to let your partner know your desires. You should practice letting your desires known when you are dating. It's okay to say "For my birthday this year I would like you to buy me flowers and take me out to dinner." This way you are letting your wishes be known and by doing so you are not cheating yourself out of a blessing that he may give you.

Chapter 19

Is He Patient?

Make sure that your prospective mate is patient. Patience is not only a virtue (good thing) but also is a test of maturity. I have happen to have dated several young men in the past who where in such a "big hurry" to get married that they not only married the wrong person but also brought a lot of heartache upon themselves. I remember one young fellow whom I dated my junior year of high school and by the time I graduated from high school, he met and married a gal he met at Bible College. Four children later, she left him for her boss she met at the bank that she worked at and left him devastated! So remember to find someone who wants to take the time to get to know you as an individual not just one bent on a conquest to marry the first gal who will marry him!

Chapter 20

Encountering Conflict

Remember that all relationships have conflict at one point or another. It's better to find this out sooner than later. Often, God Almighty gets us to see the conflict in others sooner to avoid heartache down the road later. If you notice any what I refer to as "red lights" early in the relationship, break it off immediately. If your date persists on being with you, either call your pastor or call the police to make a police report. There are laws that prevent individuals from stalking one another.

On the other hand, if he has broken off the relationship, don't try to pursue it any further. Remember that time heals all wounds. Also, the same laws that apply to you also apply to him. After all, you wouldn't want to be with someone who doesn't accept you or love you for you. You will eventually get over him, trust me!

However, not every disagreement we encounter with our prospective mate has to be solved at that moment. At times we can agree to disagree. If you cannot agree to disagree, you can walk away from the argument, cool down, and then reproach as if nothing ever happened. My Dad use to have a saying that had some truth to it; he often said, "The less said, the quicker mended." My Dad actually said that he got that saying from his mother. The point is simple: forgive your lover and time will heal all wounds. You don't always have to vent your words and emotions!

Learn how to be able to have conflict with him in a healthy way. Allow conflict to bring you closer to each other emotionally. By this, I do not mean yelling at him or calling him names. I mean communicate your needs, wants, and expectations in a healthy way by using an "I" message (VIEW CHAPTER #57 BELOW).

Once you are married to your prospective mate, there will inevitably be conflict. Be careful to figure out which wars are worth waging. Arguments take a lot out of you both emotionally. That doesn't mean that one of you must give into the demands of the other. You should both agree on a solution that is certifiable to both of you. Save your energy on the fights that move you forward as a couple, not on the ones that leave you in tears! In the end, you will have much more to give to each other.

Chapter 21

Dating a Well-Respected Man

Marry a man who is well respected in the community. If you want to know about a man's reputation, ask another man who knows him well in the church, preferably your pastor. Men, generally speaking, can evaluate the character of other men well. Although, I have done this in the past, I have found that people can either be wrong about others or unwilling to say anything derogatory about another person. So you have to rely a lot on the voice of the Holy Spirit.

Chapter 22

Dating a Kind-Hearted Man

Make sure that you marry a man who is kind-hearted. Although this may seem obvious, remember that men often put their best foot forward when dating. Only time will tell his true character. As I Corinthians 13:4–8 states that: "Love is patient, love is kind. It does not envy, it does not boast, it is not proud. It is not rude, it is not self-seeking, it is not easily angered, it keeps no record of wrong. Love does not delight in evil but rejoices with the truth. It always protects, always trusts, always hopes, always perseveres. Love never fails."

Some things to keep in mind are: Does he open the car door for you? Does he open other doors for you? Does he pay your way to dinner or insist on you paying your own way? Does he pay you a compliment once in awhile? For your sake, I hope the answer to these questions is an atonishing "yes."

Marriage is a lot of work. It not only fills your mind but also demands your time and effort into pleasing your partner. The more that you want to do for him simple things like mending his clothes or baking him his favorite kind of pie, the more he will want to please you as well. Marriage is a reciprocal relationship.

For example, I remember my first husband working at a pizza parlor during our first year of marriage. I love pizza! My husband also knows that I would love for him to bring home a large ham and pineapple pizza after his shift.

What I did not know then that I now know is that eating pizza three or four times per week will put a lot of weight upon oneself! The point is simple, however, that the more he wanted to please me; the more I wanted to do for him in return!

Chapter 23

Respecting Authority

Make sure he gets the permission of your parents' before marrying you. This is a sign that he respects authority. You see, before you marry, you are still under your parents' authority. I had my first husband ask my Daddy for my hand in marriage before I married him. He honored me for honoring my earthy father.

If your Dad is deceased obviously you cannot get his permission to get married. You can either have your prospective mate ask your mother for your hand in marriage or direct him to your church pastor for permission in marrying you. Either way it will prove to him that you do respect authority. However, this step should not take place of the other four steps to God's will as outlined in Chapter #25 below.

Chapter 24

Communicating Well

Marry a man who communicates well. If he is able to express his feelings, this is a good sign. Also, if he can communicate well before marriage, he will communicate well after marriage. When problems arise such as health problems or money problems, if you can communicate well, it will make it easier for the both of you. Remember, however, that communication does not come naturally and must always be worked on.

Chapter 25

The 5 Steps to the Will of God

Remember to apply the 5 STEPS TO THE WILL OF GOD in considering a lifetime partner. They are:

1. WANT TO; I must want to do the will of God; this is a prerequisite for the others.

2. Holy Spirit; I must have the peace of God before marrying him.

3. God's Word: The Word of God must confirm that he is the one for me to marry.

4. Open/Closed Doors: God will open and close the appropriate doors for me.

5. Godly Council: This refers to others I respect in the community, such as pastors, elders, etc.

Chapter 26

Loyalty

Make sure that he has unconditional loyalty to you. If he is loyal to his family of origin, he will generally by loyal to the family he has married into. Although this is a general guideline to follow, it is not true in every situation. Therefore, getting to know him over a period of time will be the key to knowing if he is a loyal guy.

It is thrilling to know that your prospective partner only has eyes for you. Your partner's undivided attention is a thing to rejoice in! You and your partner are all there is at this moment in time! You are exclusive to each other. Let your prospective mate pay you this compliment of being the recipient of his undivided attention!

Chapter 27

Developing Interest Independently

Make sure that he has outside interests. Nothing could be more boring if all of his interests were my interests. In fact, my first husband was like this. Because I liked collecting porcelain dolls and computers and I had an interest in fish, he also developed my interests and never had any real interests of his own. Although I enjoyed the time we two shared in going to the fish store together, I often wished that he was more independent, driving to the fish store and computer store himself.

Be sure your taking an interest in his interests is real and not feigned. If you will never love computers, don't suffer in silence when he takes an interest in purchasing a motherboard. Your partner will sense your falseness and will loose trust in you over time.

Chapter 28

Dating a Spirit-Filled Man

Make sure that your prospective man is spirit-filled. Nothing could be worse than being married to a carnal man. By this I mean to make sure of two things: That he is a soul-winner and a prayer warrior. Then you will not go wrong. As Ephesians 5:11 states: "Have nothing to do with the fruitless deeds, of darkness, but rather expose them."

Chapter 29

Developing a Relationship With God

This one should be your #1 priority in your own life. It is for you to develop an intimate relationship with the Lord. Don't play games with God and others. Ask Jesus what He wants of you in ministry and do it! If your church will not allow you to do what you feel lead to do, it's time to find another church. Don't let others get in your pathway of finding peace with God! As James 4:8 states: "Come near to God and He will come near to you."

Chapter 30

Developing Mutual Respect

Make sure that you both have mutual respect for one another. If you do not respect your date for whatever reason, don't marry him! It will only get worse! Likewise, if he makes sexual remarks to you or asks you for sex, then he does not honor you as a creature made in the image of God Almighty! (Genesis 1:27). Sex should only be discussed between marriage partners only!

Chapter 31

Forgetting "Old Flames"

When you are out on your date with your prospective mate, do not talk about other men you have dated in the past nor your ex-husband. This is a sign that you are either not over your emotional hurt of the past or hung up on another guy. Either way this is a sure way to spoil something that might have been. I have been on both sides of this fence so I know from experience that it is a BIG MISTAKE to do!

Others, on the other hand, may not agree with me and may feel that to reveal whom you have dated in the past may be a good way of getting to know someone better and vice versa. By vice versa I mean that opening up may get them to know you better as well, according to those who have a different viewpoint than I do. Therefore, you must decide this one for yourself after much prayer and a leading of the Holy Spirit.

If you do decide to discuss past flames with your prospective mate as a way of him getting to know you better, be sensitive to his feelings. Do not reveal previous sexual partners at all. Be careful not to hurt his ego.

Chapter 32

Age Factors

Date and marry someone in your own generation. Sure older men sometimes have more money but money is not the glue that holds together a marriage. It is a lot of love, commitment and hard work that holds it together. You want someone you can relate to and that would be someone in your own age bracket. Also, you need to take into consideration life-expectancy factors when dating a gentleman much older than you. If he is the primary breadwinner and you both have children together, this should be taken into consideration as to who will care for the children when he passes away.

Chapter 33

Putting Away "Vices"

Don't date someone who is addicted to cigarettes, alcohol, or gambling. These are symptoms of a much-deeper problem that you are not qualified to solve. The money that is used on these habits is unnecessarily wasted. Financial problems are one of the most common reasons for divorce in the United States.

Chapter 34

Humility Counts

You want to date and marry a man who is gentle, not harsh with you. Since he is to exemplify Christ, he should be as gentle and humble in heart as Christ was. If he is too proud to apologize for making a mistake, then he is neither humble nor gentle. Only through getting to know him over time will you be able to tell if he is humble enough to apologize for his mistakes. After all, making mistakes is human for all of us and impossible to avoid.

Chapter 35

Responsibility Counts

Date and marry a man who is responsible. In other words, does he show up on time for work everyday? Find out if he pays his bills on time. This may mean extra time invested in getting to know him but the payoff will be worth it. Also, you may have to get his permission to run a credit report on him. I wish that I had done this the first time around because I found out that my first husband had a lot of debt that affected me as well!

Chapter 36

Marriage is Not a "Cure -All"

Realize that marriage does not solve your problems, especially your financial problems. If you are lonely, it could temporarily solve loneliness. But don't look at marriage as an escape but rather as a base with two healthy individuals wanting to start a family together. Then, you will not marry the wrong person.

Marriage can often be a lonely place as well. There are times when you will feel misunderstood or unappreciated by the man whom you love the most. There is no more despairing feeling than to know that your man who has pledged to be beside you until death does not care about you at this moment in time. Only the remembrances of the happy times that the two of you have shared will keep you going during this time.

Chapter 37

Prayer Counts

PRAY, PRAY, PRAY! Pray to God Almighty about the qualities that you'd like to see in a mate. Give the outcome of whom He brings into your life to HIM! As the Word says, "Pray continually" (I Thessalonians 5:17).

Chapter 38

Forgiveness Matters

Date and marry a forgiving husband! We all sin and make mistakes; I want a man who can overlook my faults! As scripture states, if I forgive my brother when he sins against me, God will forgive me my sins!

As Matthew 6:14–15 states: "For if you forgive men when they sin against you, your heavenly Father will also forgive you. But if you do not forgive men their sins, your Father will not forgive your sins" . A bitter, unforgiving attitude can also ruin God's plan for your life.

Once you are married, you need to be bigger than your hurt, inner child. True forgiveness must occur. You must let go of your ego. True forgiveness gets your eyes off of yourself!

Practice forgiveness. Nothing is worse than a bitter, unforgiving countenance. Forgiveness is a process started by making a choice to forgive. The results of forgiveness are an inner joy and peace. Forgiveness is a vital ingredient for any relationship, particularly a marriage relationship!

Start today by making choices to forgive those who have hurt or disappointed you. This will not only make you an attractive person on the outside but also an attractive person on the inside as well as you will become easier to communicate with. It is almost impossible to communicate well with a bitter person. Each time that you learn to forgive those who hurt you, you will become closer to God. God, in return, can forgive you your sins!

Chapter 39

Ministry Matters

Get involved in the same ministry together as a way to get to know your intended better. For example, if you both enjoy singing in the choir or teaching Sunday school, then do it together. It will not only bring you together on a spiritual level, but also you will see how your intended handles situations and people. This may seem like your investing a lot of effort in getting to know him, but the results will be the pay for you in the end.

You should act in the area of your spiritual gifts. For example, if your gift is teaching, then you should teach a Sunday school class together. However, if you cannot carry a tune then I don't suggest that you and your prospective mate join the church choir. On the other hand, if your intended spouse is a bus driver for your church then I would suggest you getting your special license to drive the church's bus so you can be with him more often!

Chapter 40

Being "Equally Yoked"

If you are a born-again christian, you must date only and marry only a born-again christian. It's like trying to mix oil and water, it just doesn't work. As 2 Corinthians 6:14 states "Do not be yoked together with unbelievers. For what do righteousness and wickedness have in common? or what fellowship can light have with darkness?"

Chapter 41

Being "Upfront"

If you really like a guy, let him know it. You can accomplish this two ways: either verbally telling him or showing him by your actions, flirting with your eyes, smiling, or playing with your hair while talking to him. You can often tell by your actions but at times, its best to just tell him that you like him in case of doubts. Also, when he calls you on the telephone, talk to him politely and be careful that you do not hung up the telephone on him without saying goodbye first. Be polite and always put your best foot forward.

Chapter 42

Exchanging Numbers

Give him your phone number or exchange telephone numbers. Ask him to call you. You don't have to sit by the telephone day and night waiting his call. After all, you have a life to live also. And if he really cares for you, he will call again if you are not home. (Unless he's really shy and you wouldn't want someone that shy because that shows insecurity).

Chapter 43

Hinting Around

If you decide that he's a shy guy and you still like him, drop a suggestion like "When are you going to finally ask me out?" OR "I'm still waiting for your phone call." Be patient because If he's still interested, he will come around eventually! When he does finally come around, just make sure that you both look and act your best. Allow him to take the initiative in asking you out, as the man is to be the leader of the home. If for some reason he cannot take the initiative in asking you out but he still shows interest in you, I'd consider this a sign that he has too many emotional hang-ups from the past and I'd move on with somebody else!

Chapter 44

Male and Female Differences

Realizing the major differences between men and women will put you ahead in the game of love. Despite the obvious biological differences, men, in general, are more task-oriented whereas women are more relationship-oriented. Therefore, until you've both discovered that you like one another, the female may have to extend more effort in the relationship. If, however, you find out that you are putting in much more effort than he is, it's time to back off and reflect if this is going anywhere at all! For example, if you are doing the entire telephone calling and he never calls you, time to halt!

Chapter 45

Being Bold

If you've discovered that your guy likes you but just is to shy to ask you out, you can try asking him out. If you do ask him out, but he tells you that he prefers doing the asking either ask him when he plans on doing it or just forget him entirely. I think that you just discovered a difficult person to deal with so maybe it's time to look elsewhere. I mean that if you've tried asking him out, hinting that he asks you out, and waiting on him to ask you out, then maybe he is just too shy for you or is plain just not interested anymore. Either way, it's best just to move on!

Chapter 46

Looking Your Best

Always, always eat right, exercise at least 30 minutes 3 times a week and look your best when you go into public. You never know whom you just might meet. You might strike up a conversation with someone whom you get along well with and may end up being the man you marry. ALWAYS look your best in public places.

Chapter 47

Providing "Emotional Space"

Allow your prospective to be an individual. Respect his privacy and provide emotional space. He, in turn, should provide you with emotional space. Do not smother each other by either calling or seeing each other everyday while you are dating. I remember when I was dating my first husband and he would want to see me everyday. It just got to be too much on me emotionally and I had to set a boundary that I would only be willing to talk to him 3 times a week. You may have to do the same thing in your relationship with your intended spouse.

Chapter 48

Entertaining Your "Inner Child"

Welcome the expression of your partner's "free child." There is a little boy/little girl in all of us. Learn how to laugh and play with each other. For example, if your man collects miniature sports cars, not only allow him to do so, but also get involved in the project with him. This will bring the two of you closer emotionally!

Indulge your partner's inner child. Let him know that you think receiving flowers is fun. Also, find out what indulges him and do it. For example, if he likes to be served champagne and breakfast in bed, indulge his whims once you are married. Practice indulging each other's whims on a regular basis.

Chapter 49

Trusting Him

Learn to trust your prospective partner. This will create an atmosphere of safety that allows partners to be open and vulnerable. However, be wary of becoming too trusting too soon in the relationship. For example, if you've only known each other for one month, you would not want to be discussing your finances with him or telling him how much money you net in a month. Trusting your partner in these areas takes months or maybe even years for some people.

Chapter 50

Recognizing His Needs

Remember that men have a desire for love and intimacy also. Intimacy takes work, however. In fact, the yearning for intimacy, for companionship, is one of man's greatest motivations. It's not conquest and it's not sexual power, but it's the desire for love.

Although sex is a major ingredient in a relationship, it is not the only ingredient. Men also want love, respect, and intimacy.

Chapter 51

Listening to Him

*M*en tend to choose their listeners' carefully. If a man shares his feelings, he, may risk scorn or rejection. Since this is too great a price to pay, he chooses his listeners' carefully or does not choose to talk at all! If, however, he does chose to open up to you on vulnerable areas such as finances, take this as a compliment that he trusts your character. Then be trustworthy of his character by not sharing this information with anyone!

Learn to be a good listener. Listening is a great catalyst for helping your partner open up to you. If you want to be understood by your partner, then put energy into understanding your partner. Listening to your prospective partner also builds trust; if you listen to him non-judgmentally, he will begin to share more secrets with you in the future.

Chapter 52

Becoming Interested in Him

Another way of getting close to your prospective is to get involved with something he loves. This may take some doing. You do not have to love the activity he enjoys, but you may be able simply to enjoy his enthusiasm. Sharing in each other's emotions will bond you together.

Chapter 53

Planning a Picnic

*M*ake his favorite foods for a picnic lunch. Stop by a local diary to purchase a hunk of cheese and a bottle of wine to bring along. Take a drive to the country. Enjoy the time just spend together alone.

Chapter 54

Forgetting the Past

When in a disagreement with your intended, don't bring up the past. Old wounds may be on your mind, but their insertion into the here-and-now will muddy the water! Learn to deal with the present issue. Although it may be tempting to bring up past issues, they really haven't any relevance to the present issue at hand.

Let go of the past. It is a true fact that if we do not understand our past, we usually end up repeating it. It is important to forgive and forget the hurts that have been done to you as well as the hurts that you have caused to others. As 2 Corinthians 5:17 states that "Therefore, if anyone is in Christ, he is a new creation; the old has gone, the new has come." Never give up your hope in Christ and in a fresh start for the future.

Remember, however, that change will only happen with our permission. We should not change for other people or we may start to feel resentful towards the people that we are changing for. We should change only for ourselves and for God!

Chapter 55

Physical Intimacy

Do achieve a certain level of physical intimacy. Set up your guidelines between the two of you and do not cross the line, even if it means loosing your date! For example, you might both agree on a French kiss before saying goodnight may be as far as you both are intending to go. Discuss this with your partner. Don't put yourself into compromising situations such as a dark, parked car! Agree ahead of time between the two of you as to how far you are willing to go. Do not compromise your values for anyone!

Chapter 56

Respecting Your Man

Respect your man. When in an argument, avoid name-calling or character assassination. This will only cause hurt feelings and put him on the defensive. If, for example, you were angry with your partner for not meeting your expectations, it would be better to use an "I" message than to yell at him. In other words, tell him how you feel by getting in touch with your true feelings or what I refer to as your "inner self." Following this guideline will help you to avoid any regrets you could encounter in the future.

Chapter 57

Communicating an "I" Message

When you communicate a message, make sure you communicate an "I" message and not a "you" message. An "I" message usually has three components: feelings, behavior, and impact. I feel__(feeling)___________ when (Behavior) because (Impact). For example, I feel lonely much of the time because you work so much and I would like to have some one-on-one time with you each day.

Chapter 58

Confronting in "Love"

Confront your partner in love. If he hurts you, you need to be real with him. Unexpressed feelings accumulate and begin to rule our inner lives. When negative feelings are stockpiled, they slowly poison our relationships. Don't nag; he will change without your nagging. Create a climate where change will be inevitable.

Chapter 59

Thinking First

Think before you speak. Before you communicate your message, slow down and think out what you are trying to say. You might find it helpful to bounce your message off a third party whom you trust and can give objective feedback to you. You don't want to say the wrong thing because things said in haste can never be erased!

Chapter 60

Taking Life in Phases

Take life in phases. We never stay where we are. Change is inevitable. And if you plan for change, the present can be much more enjoyable. Start by taking steps, even small steps, toward opportunity. For example, my goal has always been to publish my own book of poetry. However, I can begin by publishing one of my poems that everyone seems to enjoy "*White As Snow*" by Tina Louise Ristine on an individual basis. In other words, learn to enjoy the simple things of life, like precious moments spent with loved ones.

Chapter 61

Having Goals

Set goals, both short-term and long-range for yourself. By long-term, I mean in 5 years or more; by short-term, I mean goals that can be achieved anywhere from 6 months to 1 1/2–2 years maximum. If you have only general, long-range goals, you will never see your goals come to pass. For example, if my long-range goal is to publish a 360-page hardback novel then my short-range goal could be to publish a soft cover version by writing 2 chapters per week for the next 52 weeks. Another example of a long-range goal may be to be married to a godly husband with 2 children: a boy and a girl within 5 years. Therefore, my short-term goal is to find someone who not only has a similar goal, but also to begin dating that person seriously.

Hold onto your dreams once you are married. Staying in touch with your goals will give you a framework to live each day. It also will make your marriage grow and thrive, as you will be adding a new dimension to the entity of your marriage.

Once you are married, you should have shared dreams together. Some couples benefit from writing down their both short-term and long-range goals on paper. If one of you is a planner and the other one is spontaneous this may not be realistic. A good point, then, will be to start in the present and the fact that you both have a goal to be married and start a family. Work from this present point to create a future plan.

Develop your own interest while waiting for God to bring Mr. Right into your life. Take a college course, publish a poem, sing in your church's choir, or take a horseback riding lesson. The more interesting you are, the more you will attract someone who is interesting to you as well! In other words, learn to develop outside interests.

In developing your own outside interests, find a solitary place where you can think, dwell, or dream without interruptions from others. Make it a point to go to this solitary place often on a regular basis away from your work, home, and your partner. In this quiet place, stay a few minutes past the time when you think that it's time to leave. Continue in

lengthening the amount of time you allow yourself
to be alone.

83

Chapter 62

Discussing Children

If you desire to have children one day, make sure that your intended spouse feels the same way! If you love children but he does not like children then you both are in for a rude awakening! Discuss these issues in advance to saying "I DO." Make sure you both agree upon having or not having children. This may seem trivial now, but I know of couples who broke up before the altar because she wanted kids and he did not want children.

Chapter 63

Being Kind

Start turning resentment into kindness. Learn to pray for and bless those who hurt you. An important step to health is acting out our beliefs to strengthen them. For example, if your brother in Christ has deeply wounded you, instead of ignoring him, go out of your way to be friendly to him. In other words, if you want friends, you must show yourself friendly.

Chapter 64

Practice Mutual Submission

Practice mutual submission. Believers should communicate with each other and submit to one another literally "In the fear of God." Whereas submission is a vertical relationship between ruler and servant, mutual submission is a horizontal relationship between equals. It also should be the attitude of husbands and wives who are believers.

Chapter 65

Praying Together

Take the time to pray together as a couple. Also you can start devotions together; there are several books out there for couples. You do not need to wait to be married to start doing devotions and praying together. This will be a building block for your future together as a couple. As the saying goes, "A family that prays together stays together". (author unknown) BE CONSISTENT in your prayers and devotions.

Chapter 66

Renewing Your Mind

Renew your mind. Maybe you've given up hope that things can change. But things can begin to change even now, beginning with the renewing of your mind. As Romans 12:2 states: "Do not conform any longer to the pattern of this world, but be transformed by the renewing of your mind. Then you will be able to test and approve what God's will is—His good, pleasing, and perfect will" . Learn to think and plan happy, positive thoughts. Begin thinking happy, positive thoughts today!

Chapter 67

Having a Sense of Direction

*H*ave a sense of direction. Proverbs 29:18 states "Where there is no revelation, the people cast off restraint; but blessed is he who keeps the law." When we have some insight into God's overall purposes in the world and sense the manifestations of His Will, we have a sense of direction. I may not have it all together, but God is working in me and I am learning and growing!

Chapter 68

Exercise the Gift of Choice

Exercise the gift of choice. We all must do things we do not enjoy such as emptying the garbage or washing the dishes or paying the bills. But no one must live an entire life they do not want to live. When you feel that you have no choice that you are unavoidably stuck in your dilemma, then you're in a dead-end role. And your feeling of not having a choice is not based on truth. You do have a choice and you alone are responsible for your own choices.

Chapter 69

Family Time

Both of you take the time to develop good relationships with both sides of your family. Remember, when you marry, you do in essence marry the family as well. Family's help is extremely important. Cherish the time spent with both sides of your families. Rotate time spent with your family. In other words, if you spend Thanksgiving with your side of the family, spend Christmas with his side of the family.

Chapter 70

Apologizing

Don't be afraid to say "I'm Sorry." When you have put your foot in your mouth and said something that you should not have said, hurt feelings will result on the part of your intended spouse. Remember that he is not made out of iron so two of the most important words in the English language now are "I'm Sorry." God will bless you for your humility. Try avoiding making the same mistake twice.

Chapter 71

Don't Forget to Say, "I Love You"

Don't be afraid to share your true feelings. The three most heart-felt words are "I LOVE YOU." Do be real, however, and say it only if you mean it. Men have a way of detecting phoniness. You may be surprised how far these three words will get you!

Chapter 72

Friends Before Lovers

Start out as friends first. In other words, become friends before becoming lovers. Taking the time to cultivate a plutonic friendship will in the long run pay off. After all, none of us lives in our sexual organs alone; we were created in 3 parts: spirit, soul, and body. Get to know the soul of another person first.

Chapter 73

Stimulate Your Thinking

Date and marry a man who stimulates your thinking ability. By this, I do not mean one who challenges your moral beliefs but one who encourages you to use your mind in expressing your God-given talents. For example, if you have the gift of teaching, he may challenge you to invent new ways for your students to memorize and understand what you are teaching them. You, in turn, should stimulate his thinking ability and challenge him to new heights that he has never gone before!

Chapter 74

Recognize the Curse

Recognize the curse put on mankind. Because of Adam and Eve's fall in the garden, the roles of men and women are often confusing. They are not what God Almighty originally intended. After the curse, God told Eve, that "Your desire will be for your husband and he will rule over you" (Genesis 3:16b). No longer is Eve an equal to Adam; Adam now becomes the boss of Eve. This not only refers to the dependency upon your future husband for daily needs but also your prospective mate will eventually become the "boss" in the relationship! This original curse translates to all husband-wife relationships forever!

Chapter 75

Becoming Friendly

Become friendly. If you want to have friends you must show yourself to be friendly. In other words, become interested in others. They, in turn, will become interested in you.

Allow your new husband to associate with his male friends. This may mean more to him than it does to you; however, we all need emotional space apart from one another. When he is out with his guy friends, you could use this time to bake a batch of chocolate chip cookies and share it with all of his male friends. This way you can adopt his friends as your own friends and not feel isolated from your man.

Another suggestion in order for you to get to know your husband's male friends is to create a unique relationship with them outside of your relationship with your husband. Call up your husband's friends just to talk or send them a greeting card just from you alone.

Chapter 76

Appreciating Uniqueness

Date and marry a man who appreciates your uniqueness. Everyone is unique and only one of you in the world has your exact fingerprints. Your intended will love you for you, not wanting to change you. Remember that there is no such thing as "normal" and if he genuinely loves you, he will not want to put you down for being different from the others.

Chapter 77

Educational Background

Date and marry a man who has a similar educational background as you do. If one of you has an 8th grade education and the other one has a master's degree, you will not be compatible with one another. You may even get frustrated in conversations. You want someone who is as educated as you are.

Chapter 78

Romance Counts

Date and marry a man who has a "romantic" side to him. Romance will fade over time so this is a good place to start out at. For example, does he buy you flowers periodically? Does he kiss your hand frequently? And does he take you for romantic walks along the beach? Does he take you to a candlelight dinner with a bottle of wine occasionally? I hope that your answer to these questions is "yes" for your sake! Romance will fade over time so it's best to start out at this level. These little gestures all add up in the game of love.

Chapter 79

Practice Hospitality

Practice hospitality. Hospitality is the art of entertaining others in your home. Don't limit it to just men. Taking the time to cultivate healthy female relationships you trust can also help improve your chances of meeting and marrying Mr. Right. Perhaps a female friend may introduce you to Mr. Right.

Chapter 80

Practice Love

Practice the art of love. Remember "Love is patient; Love is kind" (I Corinthians 13:4). To find someone who is loving and appealing to you, you must also love others. I'm suggesting a consistent, predictable offering of grace, a lifestyle of kind gestures and words. If you see someone who needs a smile, try smiling at him or her first. It takes more muscles to frown than to smile anyway. If a friend of your is in a crisis, offer a helping hand or often just a gesture of sending flowers or a greeting card can brighten his/her day!

Chapter 81

Developing Empathy

Develop empathy for others. Remember that not everyone has walked in your shoes nor have you walked in their shoes. Even if, for example, you have not had to experience the loss of a parent dying, you can consol a friend by remembering that death is inevitable for us all. On the other hand, if you have experienced the loss of a loved one, you can more easily put yourself in another person's shoes! There is an old familiar saying that goes like this "If you can help, help or at least do not hurt one another in the midst of their storm or crisis" (author unknown).

Chapter 82

Becoming a Quality Person

The key to remember is that you need to also be that quality person that the man is seeking. He may also have his list of qualities that he prays over and is dedicated to. Therefore, if you need to make any changes in your appearance or personality then do it now. Remember that the only one that can change you is YOU!

Before you decide to marry your prospective partner, make a list of the things that you want from your marriage or qualities that you want to see in your prospective mate. Make sure that your list is realistic. Cross out any qualities that your prospective mate does not have. Decide on the qualities that are most important and concentrate on those. There are only so many qualities that you can strive for in a mate.

Chapter 83

Time Heals All Wounds

If you are dating a gentleman who has come from a recent divorce, remember that it takes about 2 years to heal from the wounds of a divorce. I advise that you wait at least 2 years after the divorce is final to begin dating. I know this seems like a lot of time but healing does take time. You do not want someone who is on the rebound who is not ready for another relationship and is not over his former spouse. I am speaking from my own personal experiences now.

Chapter 84

Marry a Godly Man

Date and marry a man who will obey God in spite of the circumstances. I think of the story of Jonah in the Bible and how, at first, he did not go to Nineveh to preach to the people as God instructed him to do. As a result, he ended up in the belly of a whale. Finally, he did obey God and preach to the people of Nineveh. You want a man who will obey God if not the first time around but at least the second time around. Also, you want a man after God's own heart like King David in the Old Testament was!

Chapter 85

Divorce Yourself

Remember that you can never be happily married to your prospective mate until you get a divorce from yourself. Successful marriage requires a certain death to self. Unless you are ready to do this, don't get married until you are! Selfishness is not only sin but also is destructive to building a healthy family.

Selflessness on both of you is the key to holding together your marriage. Both parties must work for the good of the whole. In other words, the two of you working together as a team is greater than each of you are alone.

Chapter 86

Marriage Is a Lot of Work

Remember that a successful marriage is not a gift. Successful marriage is achieved by a lot of love, commitment, and self-sacrificial hard work! Successful marriage is achieved over time. It is worth the time and work that it takes however! And it is a lot less painful than what divorce brings!

Chapter 87

Physical Attraction

*R*emember that physical attraction is a beautiful thing but it is not love. Do not confuse physical attraction with love. What love requires on top of instant emotion is time, shared, happy experiences, and a long bond between two individuals. However, I do not want to minimize physical attraction because without it, the relationship could not exist!

Chapter 88

Allowing For Growth

Remember that a good marriage allows for change and growth in the individuals. Your partner will change, hopefully for the good over time. Don't waste your energy trying to change him; he will do it automatically without your nagging! I learned this guideline during my first marriage. However, the key is learning to accept your prospective mate for who he is with his faults and all! The only person that you should try to change is YOU!

Chapter 89

Love Should Be the Only Basis For Marriage

Remember that love should be the only basis for marriage. You should not marry for money, for houses, or any other status symbol but pure and simple, L-O-V-E! In other words, love and marriage should go together like a horse and a carriage! If you marry for any other reason, you will only be asking for problems in the future. Infatuation changes with time but true love will stand the test of time!

Chapter 90

Discovering Peace

If you have prayed for your prospective mate and waited for God Almighty to show you the answer if he is the one for you, remember the 5 steps to God's Will as outlined in chapter number #25 above. If you still have not any peace about marrying him, break it off with him immediately. The longer you wait to break it off, the harder it will be. Remember that the best divorce is the one that takes place before the altar! It's not too late until you say "I DO" in my opinion!

To order additional copies of

Guidelines for Finding a

Christian Husband

Have your credit card ready and call:

1-877-421-READ (7323)

or please visit our web site at
www.pleasantword.com

Also available at: www.amazon.com
www.barnesandnoble.com
www.christianbooks.com

Printed in the United States
92728LV00009B/32/A